W.A.D.E Factors

Learning to Use Your
Thoughts, Feelings and
Actions
to
Achieve Happiness and
Success

Wade Bloodgood

IbbiLane Press

copyright ©2017

All rights reserved. No part of this book may be reproduced or utilized in any form or by any means, electronic or mechanical, including photocopying, recording, or by any information storage and retrieval systems, without permission in writing from the publisher.

Cover design by Leah Frieday

ISBN-13: 978-0692833087 (IbbiLane Press)

ISBN-10: 0692833080

Acknowledgments:

I'd like to start by thanking my cross fit coach, Wendy Metzger. She was an integral part of bringing inspiration to my life, which is now playing a huge role in my future. I am forever grateful and admire you so much. You epitomize true strength, which encourages me to keep going forward every day. You are appreciated.♥

I want to thank motivational speaker Les Brown. It was one of his speeches, (which my coach Wendy Metzger shared with me) that helped saved my life and gave me the belief that I have greatness within. Mr. Brown brought spirit back into my life, when the light was dimming. I will be forever grateful.

I would like to thank Kellie Fitzgerald for giving me this opportunity to share my life work and mindset development in this book. I am very grateful and appreciate having you as my publisher. You showed up in this journey of mine at the perfect time. You are a true blessing. ♥

I would like to thank my editor, Tony Dodd. He has been a good friend for over a decade. He is one of the most talented and intelligent people I know. He can take my rambling writings and turn them into true beauty. Not an easy task! You are appreciated.

I would like to thank my son for being born and for being a blessing in my life! I am grateful for you. I love and appreciate you, DaVannis. Always! ♥

I'd like to give huge thanks, appreciation and gratitude to my best friend Carolyn Clow and her boys for all the love, and for being a part of my growth. You have taught me what it means to be a true friend, and what it means to be part of a family. You truly are the Dali Mama. ❤

Thank you to Dave Daley, the monster motivator, for the encouragement provided in his book, *"Knock Out Fear in the First Round!"* I am grateful for the timing of our paths coming together! Keep up the awesome work, brother. You are a complete inspiration.

Thank you to everyone that has stood by my side, even when it wasn't easy. I appreciate all of you for not giving up on me!

Last, but certainly not least, I am thankful and grateful for God. you made me the way I am. you never give me more than i can handle. All of the good and bad times in my life have molded me into a person I can be proud of, as I continue to set goals and achieve my dreams. This is what brought *"W.A.D.E. Factors"* to fruition.

Remember: all things are possible when you have faith. Don't EVER give up on your dreams!

Overview:

"*W.A.D.E. Factors,*" by author Wade Bloodgood, is a collection of affirmations and recommendations for developing positive life habits, which together provide a framework for better physical and mental health. It examines the theory that personal **thoughts, feelings, and actions** dictate whether one assumes an essence of negativity or positivity. By breaking down each concept into weekly, daily, and moment-by-moment timelines, the book facilitates the journey from an unhappy, unhealthy body and soul, to a life of fulfillment, self-worth and relevance. The writings are targeted to anyone who needs to correct destructive influences in their lives, or simply needs some motivation to live a healthier and happier existence.

Wade Bloodgood is an Oregon native. He is 41 years young. He is a father, a certified speaker, an outdoor survival instructor, entrepreneur, and an avid fisherman. He has a deep love for nature. Among his favorite things to do is to spend time with his three-legged dog, Seeley. His goal and purpose is to bring growth, peace and healing to all people in need.

Three years ago, Wade was 38 years old and had been told throughout his life that he would not amount to anything. He was a high school dropout and was diagnosed by doctors as having many learning disorders and conditions, such as ADHD, low language comprehension, PTSD, and a long list of others. Throughout his life, doctors, parents and teachers had failed him. He often had suicidal thoughts and tremendous amounts of depression and feelings of misery.

When he finally woke up and discovered that his negative **thoughts, feelings and actions** were the writers/creators of his life stories, he began implementing mind exercises into his daily routine. He began taking control of his life and his mind. This resulted in immediate positive change; change that continues to unfold, through the daily work and the beliefs he has put into this book.

Understanding and controlling **thoughts, feelings and actions brings** positive, life-changing results. This book will help you understand that our minds are powerful, and that we can take control of what we think, what we feel, and how we act. When we do, life will take a positive turn. It will seem as if a miracle has happened. *"W.A.D.E. Factors"* outlines the steps to help guide you to the positive energy inside you: energy that upon release will change your self-perception, instill self-worth, and result in the rejuvenated, confident, happy person you always wanted to be.

Table of Contents

Introduction   15

Chapter 1:   23
- Water and Nutrition
- All day
- Daily
- Every day

Chapter 2:   31
- Wade
- Approach
- Direction
- Excuses

Chapter 3:   37
- Want
- Attitude
- Discipline
- Evolve

Chapter 4:   43
- What
- Acquire

- Develop
- Enthusiasm

Chapter 5: 49
- Worth
- Ambition
- Desire
- Enterprise

Chapter 6: 55
- Wake up
- Actions
- Do well
- Execution

Chapter 7: 61
- Work
- Accomplish
- Determination
- Energy

Chapter 8: 67
- Will power
- Attraction
- Do
- Exercise

Introduction

You must exercise your mind to condition it, in order to retain its good health, and to promote positive thinking. Like a long-distance runner, you must build the stamina and endurance that you need that comes with continued non-stop efforts to elevate the journey to the next level. Get to a higher plane, and to a better life that we all were destined to live.

You must make a real attempt to catch yourself when thinking negative thoughts about the past. Unless you're willing to positively address any negative situations that have already passed, you will just be perpetuating the problem! The past serves no purpose, except to reflect as a guide to avoid the mistakes or hurdles we have already jumped, and to learn from those positive and negative experiences, and to grow, and avoid repeating the same mistakes that give us the results that most often make us unhappy. When negative self-talk is present, remind yourself that those negative thoughts serve you no purpose, and then replace them with positive thoughts. Remind yourself what you are grateful for. You are worthy. You are loved. Tell yourself: I am a conscious and aware person. I have choices. I choose positivity, and the negative thoughts and feelings are not welcome here and must leave immediately!

Practice as much as you can. The more you are consciously aware of what you are spending your time thinking about, the more you will discover the things upon which you are wasting precious life/time: things that you cannot control or change in the past, present, or future. We must remain true to ourselves and redirect towards the positive life path. It is hard work at first! No one walks into a gym and lifts 500 lbs. It takes time to build up to that level. It takes dedication and time, doing the work, growing, and learning, to push yourself to the next level, until lifting 500 pounds is much easier to accomplish. The process to success is difficult, but it is worth the effort. What you need to do to get there is to start the journey, and visualize the destination, and then do it, bit by bit, never looking back. Regardless of the growing pains, which are worth every bit of your life to feel and experience the sweat, tears and blood that your heart beats. Your mind and body are moving as one in action: showing you that because you earned it, and that you understand it, and that you believe in yourself, and the process of all it is and how it works.

Tell yourself: I am loved! I am worth it! I am all that I dream! I have proved to myself that I will achieve and succeed under any conditions thrown at me! I will rise above the negative, the odds against me and I will laugh knowing that I have prepared myself to not ever fear failure. There is nothing to be afraid of except NOT DOING IT! DO NOT GIVE UP ON YOUR LIFE! Exercise your **thoughts, feelings and actions,** because living a life full of negative, unhappy, unsuccessful unachieved dreams, goals, passions or desires is a wasted way to spend one's existence. You were born with a purpose. Small or big: you have a calling.

What is your reason?
Every day, you need to ask yourself: "What is my reason?" Know all the positives that lead to achieving your goal. Recognize the different factors you have applied that have quickly changed your life. If it feels and looks better, remember, and DO IT AGAIN. On days that you feel negativity, it is a perfect opportunity to reapply these positives and to exercise your mind, pushing you to a higher level!

Every day is a new day to exercise your mind. This is a non-stop process for the rest of your new life! Be conscious of what you spend your time thinking about and be aware of the things you are and are not doing. Exercise your mind. Keep a positive mindset. Gain confidence within yourself that will align your **thoughts, feelings and actions,** leading you to the **life that you most want to live.** Avoid the nightmare that has become what some have accepted: miserable existences, as if there is no hope, powerless to change what is happening in their lives. YES, YOU CAN AND WILL DO SOMETHING BIG!

First, catch your negative thoughts and redirect your thinking to something positive. That can be achieved through reciting words, like calm, peace, love, healing, grateful, or by recalling a happy memory. Tell yourself that you are worthy, and that you are loved! You will achieve the life that you dream of. Every time your mind slips into negative thoughts. STOP! Catch yourself and redirect to positivity. We must repeat this repeatedly. If you slip into negativity, redirect your thoughts to positivity, even if it only lasts a few minutes. Repeat your positive thoughts over and over. This exercise, in time, will reprogram how your mind was stuck on all the negatives that you thought that you had no control over. They will be replaced naturally in time with positive thoughts, no matter what life throws at you!

You will begin to see all negative events in a new positive light, taking away the negative energy that is trying to get into your head! DON'T LET IT! Misery does not live here and is not welcome in your life. You have great abilities within you and you are put here for a reason, Find that purpose and achieve your dreams and live the life that you were destined to live. Start today! EXERCISE YOUR MIND. It all begins with what you put into your body.

Thoughts, feelings and actions = RESULTS.

Chapter 1

Water & Nutrition

Water is essential to all living things. Our bodies are composed of approximately 80% water. Water has the great ability to retain energy and expand that energy within itself. Our eyes cannot see this, of course! Basically, water takes on the energy of our words, sound and actions. If we have negative self talk the 80% of the water that makes up our bodies takes on this energy, producing more negative results! It's like polluted water: It is not good or safe for you to drink or to have in your body. Most of us would not consciously drink polluted water, which we knew would make us sick or bring negative results to our lives. So: first we must replace the negative **thoughts, feelings and actions** with positive **thoughts, feelings and actions**, as we practice this positive thinking exercise. Then, we begin to produce and reflect the positives back into our lives, because the 80% water our body is made of is now positive, non-polluted, clean, fresh and healthy circulating water. Life just starts to begin to have a new happier feeling to it, creating many more positive results in our lives.

The things we put into our bodies is as important as the water and positive things we tell ourselves. What we put into our bodies can also affect our ability to stay focused on the positive in life, maintaining the positive energy levels and remaining conscious of our **thoughts, feelings and actions.** Lack of proper nutrition can allow our thoughts to stray, or make us lazy, and cause us to procrastinate. That can spiral out of control into negative **thoughts, feelings and actions**. Eating good, clean, healthy fresh foods can prevent this! It's time to stop eating (or eat as little as possible) processed foods of any kind. Read the nutrition labels for ingredients, and choose the best possible foods for you and your family's positive health and longevity. Sugars are a huge cause in cancer and disease. You are what you eat. Food fuels your entire body and your mind's engine. Do not put low-grade fuel, low-grade octane fuel, full of additives that are not good for you, in your tank! The healthier and cleaner you eat and drink, the more you will begin seeing positive things start happening in your mind, body and life!

All Day

Remember to eat well, drink clean, fresh water, and remain conscious of your thoughts. Do these things to get your life on the path of positivity and success: achieving your goals and dreams! DO NOT counteract all the positive results with negatives like drinking alcohol, taking illicit drugs, or engaging in mindless self-indulgences that do not serve you any purpose or growth. These activities will result in a negative outcome! Don't consume e-cigs, regular cigarettes, chewing tobacco, soda, fast food, or high-calorie junk food. Refrain from drinking energy drinks or other quick-fix potions they sell you at every turn! Get active, take action and become conscious, and your life will start becoming more positive, giving you the boost to believe in yourself, and in your **thoughts, feelings and actions,** producing **Positive Life Changing Results!**

Daily

Check in with yourself to see how you are doing with the mental exercises, mind-strengthening and retraining: how you think you are doing in the areas that are holding you back. Make notes of where you are struggling in the process, and what you can do that will change those outcomes. Stay vigilant. Consistency is what will produce success! Write down your progress, so that over time, you can see and measure how far you have taken yourself from a negative to a positive life. In time, as we actively remain focused and conscious, we learn to align our positive thoughts with our positive feelings, creating our positive outcomes. As we master this, we will begin to overcome fears, and find endless wisdom, peace & happiness. This is a big part of achieving; a process which all W.A.D.E. Factors can help to educate ourselves to obtain what we want and need to know to accomplish passion and attain goals and dreams. Things won't change from the couch or while sleeping! You have to engage by action!

Every Day

Every day, we need to remain conscious of what our **thoughts, feelings and actions** are producing, and the effects they have on the lives around us. We need to always attempt to catch our negative comments and replace them with positive, productive solutions: to stay aware of our path. We need to be able to recognize others that are also on our path, and most importantly, realize the ultimate responsibility we have in the results of the path we have chosen.

Sometimes, you have to choose to let go of those people, places or things that you realize are holding you down or not positively supporting the greater good for your life. It's tough to have to let go of people and letting them figure out for themselves how to be happy and achieve their goals or dreams. Remember: that is your job for yourself. This is for you to stay focused on your path: not looking at anyone else, or requiring the approval of anyone else. It is okay for you to be living a positive, happy, self-worthy existence: achieving your passions, goals and dreams! It will be hard at first, because doing the right and positive thing has become a lot harder than we initially thought! Exercise and practice. It will become second nature as you grow, with non-stop conscious **thoughts, feelings and actions** that produce **our results.** You will begin to notice that you are making healthier, more positive and productive friends, and experiencing positive life events. Suddenly, you will be handling yesterday's stresses and false worries as if they are a gift that help keep you sharp and stay strong in your beliefs, and restore your faith in your ability to create your own outcomes by using your God-given talent of mastering your **thoughts, feelings and actions.**

Chapter 2

Wade: (verb) To walk through water or something else that impedes normal movement. To cross or pass through with difficulty. To plunge into, or to begin or attack resolutely and energetically.

In life, we will all encounter hardships and difficult situations and tough choices. Be prepared for this, and be ready to walk through anything that tries to impede you from moving towards your wants/goals/dreams/passions, by facing your fears and attacking it with all that you have, as if your life depends on it. Be prepared to expend the energy to overcome, go over, go around, go under, or smash straight through anything that is in your way of what you want out of life. As you learn and apply the W.A.D.E. factors, you will be able to achieve anything you want, regardless of what gets in your way. Let's start wading!

Approach: (noun) A way of dealing with something.

How you approach a situation is entirely up to you. If you approach it with a closed/negative mind, you will most likely get unwanted results. If you approach the situation with an open/positive outlook, the probability is that you will achieve the desired outcome. In order to be accomplished, we need to first look at our approach: How is this affecting me? Is this good or bad for me? Does this feel right or wrong? What am I willing to do to get the results I desire? If even a tiny part of you knows that a situation is wrong, or does not feel healthy or positive, DO NOT DO IT! Too often, we completely ignore that inner voice and instinct. We have made doing "what is right" so difficult in our minds that we simply allow negative things right on in, pretending to be happy with it, because that's the way it is. NO IT IS NOT! STOP THIS THINKING TODAY! Change your approach and "that's just the way it is" attitude. The "way it is" is how you make it.

Direction: (noun) A course along which someone or something moves.

I want you to stop! Look around. Where are you? Be honest with yourself. Look at the path upon which you are proceeding. Do you see it leading to where you want to be in life? Is it a positive, encouraging path? These are questions that you must ask yourself, honestly and truthfully. We all can change direction at anytime. No matter who we are, where we live, what we look like, or how much money we have or do not have. It all can start right now, in a positive motion to redirect your direction towards the positive places and the person that you want to be. Start moving forward into the life that you are destined to live. In time, you will build momentum, and achieve anything that you desire.

Excuse: (noun) attempt to lessen the blame, attaching to a fault or offense. To seek to defend or justify. To release from duty or requirement. A person or expectation put forward to defend or justify a fault or offense.

Excuses are your nightmares. In fact, all of your excuses hold you back from doing what you are destined to do for yourself. If's, and's, but's, should have, could have, would have! I am going to

do it later! Procrastination and all the excuses you make are the reasons your dreams, goals, passions, are not becoming a reality!
Many things will get in our way as roadblocks. They are not valid excuses why we cannot do whatever it takes to achieve what we want from life! Stop lying to yourself. Stop justifying your lack of action or the negative **thoughts, feelings and actions** in your life. The only fault that you are not in a more positive growth state, happy in life, achieving what you want is YOU! YOU MAKE YOUR EXCUSES. NOW MAKE THE REASONS TO GET UP OFF THE COUCH, TO WAKE UP, AND LIVE YOUR DREAMS! Stop going out drinking, partying and distance yourself from unhealthy and negative friends for one year.

Start today. A 365-day challenge to take your current circumstances and change your life direction for the better. Or, you can continue to make excuses and keep an extra room for misery to live in. Life, no matter how good it can be, will always try and punch you in the face! So be prepared when they come. Do not let them knock you down! We are fighting for our positive lives! THERE ARE NO EXCUSES. Take personal responsibility for everything that has to do with YOU. You control you! So make the choice that you need to let go of the past, and to live in the present…for the brighter future we all want. We can achieve success in anything we want, as long as we don't make excuses, thus perpetuating our own downfall.

Chapter 3

Want: (verb) To desire greatly. To wish for. To desire someone to do something.

THAT SOMEONE IS YOU! You have to greatly desire, and be willing to do whatever it takes to get what you want! No one else can or will make it happen for you. That's your work to do! Once you figure out what you want, you have to create a plan of action and focus on the task. Recognize what you want, envision it as if it has already happened or is presently happening, and then continue to do so with the feeling of positive outcome and action. The opportunity will soon arise, and then you have to continue to take non-stop positive action. Those that do not get what they want fail because they want everything, without working for it, or because they make half-attempts to satisfy the crowd. Don't worry about the crowd: it's yourself that you should worry about. This is your life! You have to work through the process to achieve what you want, or you will never accomplish your dreams. YOU CAN ACHIEVE ANYTHING IF YOU TRULY WANT AND BELIEVE IN IT, AND ARE WILLING TO DO THE WORK

Attitude: (noun) The position of the body or manner of carrying oneself. a state of mind or feeling. An arrogant or hostile state of mind. The way we carry ourselves. The way we think about ourselves. The way we feel about ourselves and set the position/direction of our body.

Attitude is not negative unless you have a negative state of mind. It has the same powerful effect as a positive attitude. In a positive view, having "attitude" means that you believe with utmost confidence, and attack life with the mindset that you have already won, and regardless of the end result, you put in 100 percent, driving forward with all that is in you, with all the belief and faith that you have. It is happening for you, and it will be done in the end. Remember to put in the hard work, and never give in or give up no matter your current results. Continue until you get the results you want and then pick up the pace!

Discipline: (noun) The practice of training people to obey rules. A branch of knowledge, typically one studied in higher education.

Discipline is what keeps us following through, combined with other important factors. Without discipline, we end up procrastinating our lives away and achieving the bare minimum. That is why the practice of training your mind and your body, and your feelings and your actions, is the rule all people should obey. This is higher knowledge: a branch of education that one should study and practice daily, as long as we discipline ourselves. We should not worry about or fear others. We should not recognize the forced rules or obey the limitations or negative implications put upon us. We have put in our time and we have dedicated ourselves. We hold ourselves accountable of our own **thoughts, feelings and actions**. The more discipline you have for yourself, with confidence and making decisions that positively benefit your life, without asking the opinion or advice of others, the more you will be rewarded with the realization of your own dreams; ON YOUR TERMS.

Evolve: (verb) To develop gradually from a simple to a more complex form.

You must free your thoughts from all that you have been taught that has led to your unfulfilled dreams and unhappiness. You must allow yourself to let go of the feelings that serve you no purpose: those that continue to hold you hostage in your own life. You must be willing to take action and allow the natural course of your evolution to take place. Development can gradually occur, or happen instantly. We will come to truly believe in our spirits, and as we evolve, we free ourselves from the negative complex form of thinking and go back to the basics, which allows us to develop a new positive complex form of ourselves. Exercise your mind and feelings. Positive actions will follow.

Chapter 4

What: (noun) The true nature or identity of something, or the sum of its characteristics.

What is a good question to ask yourself?
What do you think?
What do you want?
What are you willing to do to achieve?
What is your purpose?
What is this doing to you?
What is your daily routine?
What is your health and eating doing to you?
What are you spending your time on?
What is important to you?
What are your dreams/goals/passions?
What do you enjoy that is just for you?

This is just a short list. In each situation, you must ask yourself: What positive purpose does this serve my life? If it does not serve a positive purpose, and only brings negativity, you must take action. It is time to remove these people, places or things from your thinking and your life. You must let go of and replace the negative and redirect yourself towards positive solutions to produce positive results. Exercise your mind and regularly practice that which will lead to your desired results. Always be aware of the things that are affecting you, and the effects they have on your life. TAKE CONTROL.

Acquire: To gain possession of. To get by one's own efforts or actions. To gain through experience or exposure to something.

The reason I chose to write this book is that I wished to acquire self-growth, and in the process, to share some of the tools that helped me. The answers for me came from my personal efforts and personal experiences regarding controlling my **thoughts, feelings and actions**. You too will gain happiness through exercising your mind. You will become experienced in how to gain positive outcomes in anything you dream, by applying the natural ability we all have within to create the reality that you desire.

This is not a complicated concept. It's simple if you apply yourself to achieving your dreams. How do you acquire? By possessing non-stop consciousness of your **thoughts, feelings and actions**. If any are negative and serve you no purpose, you must let them go. Replace them with positive self-worth, love, and the **thoughts and feelings** that you DO want. It's time to take action for your life.

Develop: (verb) To grow or cause to grow and become more mature, advance or elaborate. To start to exist, experience or possess.

In order to develop, you must be willing to grow. You have to want to grow and be willing to change for positive reasons. You have to be open-minded to the idea and techniques of what this growth will do for you when applied in your **thoughts, feelings and actions.** It will result in your dreams becoming a reality. You will succeed in achieving the goals you strive for. It won't be easy. It takes everyday practice, and hard work. You must be consciously aware of your **thoughts, feelings and actions,** and exercise your mind with positivity, fully believing that you are going to fulfill your potential.

Enthusiasm: (noun) Intense and eager enjoyment, interest or approval.

We need to constantly keep ourselves in an intense mode of interest in our life goals, dreams, and passions. We need to find things we feel eager to do that bring us enjoyment and provide the positive results that we are seeking. Our attitude needs to be enthusiastic. It's contagious, and the excitement you bring with you will be seen as confident, believable, and most importantly: it will be seen as achievable. You must stay positive in your **thoughts, feelings and actions** to see the positive results. If you don't have it…GET IT! Enthusiasm will begin to change everything.

Chapter 5

Worth: (noun) The quality that renders something desirable, useful or valuable. Deserving of merit. To the utmost of one's power or ability.

It is so important that you find your self-worth and believe in who you TRULY are. No matter what others think of you. It does not serve you any purpose to concern yourself with what others think of you or how they treat you, either good or bad. The most important thing is what YOU think of YOU.

The quality of someone that evokes desirability, and is useful, lies within himself or herself. Successful people take action in the direction that leads to achieving, deserving of merit and bringing out the utmost abilities in them and utilizing their power to achieve what they desire. Build your worth by exercising your mind, and by telling yourself that you are worthy of your dreams, and settle for nothing less than your ultimate goals.

Ambition: (noun) A strong desire to do or achieve something, typically requiring determination and hard work.

You have to want it with all that you have in you. You must be willing to go through whatever it takes to achieve your dreams.
You have to begin to manifest that positive strong desire to achieve and be completely open and ready to do whatever hard work is in your way to get to where you want to be. Never regress once you get there. You have begun to master the skills and

techniques that it takes to achieve…KEEP IT UP and stay there! You must keep your tools sharp and believe in your abilities, Things become much easier and simplified. You can now pick up the pace. You made it this far. It is NOT an option to stop this mind exercising and processing positive **thoughts, feelings and actions**. Your ambition will pay off. Never stop driving forward.

Desire: (noun) A strong feeling or wanting to have something, or wishing for something to happen. A strong wish or want.

Desire exemplifies the physical feelings that we can't ignore. We wish for things to happen. Emotions make us want it so badly that we must apply action and true thought and true feelings. The desire can and will be a reality. Faith and belief… it works both ways between negativity and positivity.

Be careful of what you desire. Make sure that you prepared to receive what you want. Most of the lost opportunities that leave you feeling lost, worthless, ashamed, abandoned, stupid is because you were unprepared. The only person to blame is you. Though we all tend to point the blaming finger at someone else and redirect the focus away from ourselves. Be prepared when your wishes become a reality, because THEY WILL! They will arrive in many forms. Don't miss a desired opportunity because you are unprepared!

Enterprise: (noun) A project or undertaking, typically one that is difficult or requires effort.

You are your enterprise. You are undertaking the project of your life. Nobody else can do it for you! This requires much conscious and physical effort, and is the simplest, yet most difficult thing to live and practice. This should be your mantra when you wake every morning. The more you exercise your mind, the more it becomes first hand nature. It's easier than you think. It's all in your perspective of each given situation or event and how you approach it. Reactions and actions we can control. Don't deny yourself the greatness within you. Your willingness to reach your full potential, and to do the work to get there, will result in achieving personal happiness.

Chapter 6

Wake up: (verb) To cause to become awake or conscious. To come alive.

You are the number one reason to become alive, awake and conscious. What you want is your cause! The key is to remain aware of your conscious thoughts. If you find yourself spending time in your head, in conversations that serve you no positive purpose, you need to stop and recognize that your thinking is counter-productive, and refocus your thoughts to what you want and are productive. It takes time to exercise and practice new thinking. Do it every day, every minute, to achieve maximum results. Before you know it, you will be controlling what you want to think and will be a step closer to what you want to achieve. The more you stop the negative thoughts and refocus on positive outcomes and solutions, the more you will achieve your goals.

Action: (noun) The state or process of acting or doing something done or accomplished. Organized activity to accomplish an objective habitual or vigorous activity energy, behavior or conduct.

To achieve success, you must take immediate action…no matter your age, or who you are. You can start this very second, or when you're tired of the life results you continue to receive! The state of your mind is very important. You need to begin positively visualizing yourself doing what it takes to get what or to where you want. See yourself achieving it. Believe in it with all your **thoughts, feelings and actions**. Once you have taken the time to exercise your brain in this area, it will become your everyday instinct to live this way and you will be living in action. Your old conduct and behavior of negative talk will be replaced with the positive beliefs and life as you want to live it will become a dream come true. Document where you are and where you want to be, Make an organized step-by-step process about how to achieve your objective. Then, engage in activities with a vigorous non-stop habitual behavior of **thoughts, feelings and actions** that produce positive results. All your goals can be obtained. If at any time you stop this process, your life can go right back to the negative. You must always remain conscious of your **thoughts, feelings and actions**.

Do Well: (verb) To act in one's or the greater good's best interest.

It is important to remember why you're doing all these things every day. To "do well" reminds you that it is in your best interest to act for you and everybody else that will also be affected by your new positive outlook. Changing your thinking and lifestyle and removing all the negativity that will no longer affect you anymore, because you have exercised your mind, will increase your self-confidence and make you a happier person. That worth is powerful in a positive way and all those within your reach will be inspired to also "do well" to take care of themselves and others with a positive outlook and energy that continues to keep all of our cups with something in them.

Execution: (noun) The carrying out or putting in effect of a plan, order or course of action.

The way we take action toward a plan is important. We must exercise our minds and bodies in a manner that allows us to execute at the top of our capabilities. Take the time to learn about what you want. Find out what steps you must take to achieve, and write down a course of action. Then, concentrate your **thoughts, feelings and actions** and act in the best interest of your plan. Your execution will play a big role in your success. So, plan well. It is about to pay off, as you engage constantly toward your goals. You won't have even realized the tremendous amount of success and growth you have achieved in a short period of time, until you reflect back on your growth through the year and go over your progress.

Chapter 7

Work: (noun) Physical or mental effort or activity directed toward the production or accomplishment of something.

In order for you to achieve anything, you must first be willing, by any means necessary, to do the work. It's difficult. It's painful. Much like the gym, you feel the pain and push through that pain, no matter how hard it is, and in the end, you come out looking and feeling better for your hard work. We all have to grow through the process to get there. No one just walks into the gym breaks weightlifting records. In order for you to accomplish anything, you have to put in all of your effort, both mentally and physically. That's why it is called work! Put in as much work you have to, to get what you want, and once you get what you want…KEEP WORKING!

Accomplish: (verb) To succeed in doing. To reach the end of completion: our goals, dreams, passions, desires.

We have to first know in our thoughts that our goal is possible! We have to consistently see in our minds, us achieving no matter what it looks like around us. We will accomplish our goals when we are in our most positive self. We have to feel that we deserve our dreams. We will do whatever it takes to achieve and feel that we are worthy, loved and deserve all that we want, with zero doubt. If doubt arrives (and it will), it is the negativity that serves us no purpose. Remain aware and conscious. Stop. Replace and redirect with positive, loving

thoughts. Doing so will produce outcomes that make us feel whole, and allow us to reach full potential and happiness.

Determination: (noun) The act of figuring out or calculating. The act of officially deciding something. A quality that makes one continue to try to do or achieve something that is difficult.

You must find your determination. You need to find out exactly what you drives you to reach full potential. Plan and calculate your thoughts and feelings. Then, you must act with all of your faith and energy, no matter how difficult it becomes. You must be steadfast in your determination to achieve! It has been officially decided in your thoughts, in your feelings, and is continued through your actions. Nothing can stop you once you have set your mind and feelings into action, except yourself. Stay determined, and never stop until you get the results you desire.

Energy: (noun) The strength and vitality for sustained physical or mental activity.

You must maintain your energy. This is achieved mainly by eating a healthy diet. Reduce the "bad" things you put into your body, as these play a role in how you feel and think. Exercise your mind. Another area to be recognized is sleep. Do not waste time sleeping; time that can be utilized bettering yourself or your situation. Learn to take two short hour-long naps, and then get back up and start working towards your dreams. You only need to sleep six hours a day: broken up, or in one 6-hour block. You can regain a year's worth of work lost due to procrastination in just one week, by sleeping only 6 hours a day. Sleep less~Achieve more! That being said, always be sure to get enough rest to maintain high performance. Some may think they need more and some may think less. Six hours is more than enough sleep to energize you all day, when eating/drinking and exercising your mind and body properly.

Chapter 8

Will Power: (noun) The strength of will to carry out one's plans, wants, or decisions. The ability to control oneself and determine one's actions and results.

Will power is a very important tool to possess if you plan to achieve your goals. You have to have will power to push yourself past the limits, to challenge yourself to take it to another level, and to relinquish all that does not serve your purpose. To carry out your plan, you have to find your strengths, and believe in your abilities. Stay determined. Control your actions. At times, when you feel like you might not make it, and negative emotions wander in, do the exercises of positive thinking, and in time, you will find that you possess an unbelievable amount of will power.

Attraction: (noun) The act or capability that attracts the gravitational force exerted by one body or another.
quality of attraction.

This is by far one of the most important items on the list. On your path to achieving the life you want, you must understand that we attract what we want and also what we don't want. Attraction is the most powerful tool that proves God is within us and that if we do not exercise the faith, we will live in misery and experience continued patterns that produce constant negatives in our lives. Express your faith in all of God's glory: Realize that you and God are one in the same, and that your thoughts, feelings and actions produce the life that God intended. The life that you also intended, because it's YOU in control of your **thoughts, feelings and actions.** We gravitate towards what we think, feel, and act! Fear is the number one reason that holds us back. It's not even the fear that we should fear the most. IT IS OURSELVES! We produce the fear and doubt within ourselves. We are our own worst enemy. Admit your flaws. Ugliness. Insecurities. Get it all out in the open. If you have nothing to hide, you have nothing to fear! Worrying about things that you cannot control serves you no positive purpose, and needs to be removed and completely deleted from your thinking. This requires exercising the mind. Practice consciousness daily. Be deliberate in your thinking. Be fully aware of what you are **thinking, feeling, and doing**. Find where you can improve in this area. If you catch yourself thinking negatively, replace it with a positive affirmation. Keep up the hard work. You are off to a great start to freedom. You are doing GREAT!

This will become much easier as you practice mind-exercises daily. This process will become so much simpler to understand, to practice and to make part of a permanent lifestyle. Your mind, body, and soul will change and you WILL be living your dreams and realize your true potential. We all were born to shine!

Do: (verb) To accomplish; finish; complete: execute, perform.

DO NOT BE AFRAID TO ASK FOR HELP, GUIDANCE, OR ADVICE, FROM A POSITIVE SUPPORT SYSTEM OR PERSON. Seek out a mentor.

DO NOT give up no matter how long it takes you…no matter the ups and downs. NEVER GIVE UP! If you give up, expect to live the life you DO NOT WANT for the rest of your life.

DO NOT let your dreams and goals fall short.

DO NOT let negative events, people, places or things become your life. You will handle daily events as positively as you can, and you will keep moving forward with dignity and with your head held high.

DO NOT make excuses or procrastinate, or fail to live up to your true potential! You have the power and strength to achieve anything you set your mind too…Believe in it! Feel it coming together. Act on it to make it a reality. YOU CAN DO IT!

Exercise: (noun) Activity requiring bodily and/or mental exertion for the training or improving of one's health.

This will be my last piece of advice, and is one of the most important steps, in combination with all the others. Remember EVERYDAY, as often as you can, to EXERCISE YOUR MIND. Remember to be conscious of what you are thinking and keep the negative self-talk conversations out! Your thoughts are important. They will create your reality.

It's also important to do physical exercise, regardless of your physical condition. This helps keep your positive feelings encouraged and actions begin to build momentum. There is no excuse to not be physically active. Our minds will keep us on our toes with the practice of reversal of negative thoughts to positive **thoughts, feelings and actions.** Our bodies will do the same with physical exercise. Learn to redirect your energy towards what we need to do positively and take action in that direction.

Don't look at it as you if you can't do it! Look at every challenge as an opportunity. You've been waiting to change your life. Don't get down about your mind's tendency to stray off into negative self-talk or thoughts that serve us no purpose. You will learn and discover in a short period of time, how much you have changed for the better and relish future moments of positive results. You should be very proud. You are doing a fantastic job, doing the hard work that will bring personal freedom. It will become as easy as tying your shoelace or just waking up in the morning or eating when you are hungry. It will become first-nature for you. There will be days that you completely forget that you were ever negative, and when negative things happen (as they do in life) you will not be knocked down for the count. You will just get up, brush yourself off, and proceed forward with confidence. You will soon see, and be thankful for, the previously unseen lessons that life can bring.

"Emancipate yourself from mental slavery, none but ourselves can free our minds."

-Bob Marley

www.ingramcontent.com/pod-product-compliance
Lightning Source LLC
Chambersburg PA
CBHW072107290426
44110CB00014B/1856